HOW TO TREAT PRETTY THINGS

Poems

Teisha Dawn Twomey

Stream~Lines

an imprint of

Riverhaven

www.RiverhavenBooks.com

Published in the United States
by Riverhaven,
www.RiverhavenBooks.com

ISBN: 978-1-937588-56-4

Printed in the United States of America
by Country Press, Lakeville, Massachusetts

First Edition, 2016

Artwork by Teisha Twomey
Cover design by Janna L. Graves
Edited and designed by Stephanie Lynn Blackman
Whitman, Massachusetts

Stream~Lines, an imprint of Riverhaven
781-447-0167
www.RiverhavenBooks.com
18 Pearl Street, Whitman, MA 02382

To Lauren Catherine Twomey,
my beautiful niece and my very pulse.
When your mother first placed you in my arms,
little did we know that she was also placing you
directly into my heart.

TABLE OF CONTENTS

Coming Home

I reach below the sink, compare the proofs
of the bottles beneath. Eighty is best

and I pour the glass half full, watching
the Diet Coke turn gold, beautiful as amber.

I climb the stairs the way I am used to,
as a child tiptoeing to my bedroom.

I do not wake the man in the master bedroom,
his hands gripping the bruised arms of his woman.

I sleep above the shot-gun my mother had hidden
below my mattress and forgotten about long ago.

It waits there. No one suspects the room
with the unicorn wallpaper. I am just visiting

tonight. I have this secret beneath the surface.
I try not to roll over. Some-thing might go off.

You will find your things

under my cradle. Some will be damaged,
others, ruined. I unraveled the woven wool

of cashmere stoles, tangled your bracelets,
teethed sunglasses and gnawed on stilettos.

I shook the necklace at your collar
and those unfettered pearls rolled

beneath me. My first word suits me well,
my baby-lips draw in to begin forming it

and my tongue clicks briefly against the roof
of my mouth when I say: *Mine.*

My sticky hands open and close
like hungry sundews, curling over

what's dear to you. When you go,
you leave the door cracked

and I can hear your laugh. I want
to own this thing most of all.

Teisha Dawn Twomey

Self-Portrait at Age Seventy-Nine

I am so old, these birds could outlive me.
I am relieved by this. Like some great weight

being lifted from my chest. The one that's been bearing down
on me, demanding. My only guests are goldfinches. I am not naïve

enough to think I own them. I unlatch their bamboo doors
every morning, always honored when they stay.

I comb my silver hair away from my face, still in love
with my collarbone. I have a hundred plants I overwater,

saying each name, like a prayer:
begonia, anthurium, lilium.

Beyond the Veil

dyeing —

in the wake of spinning
each thread by hand,

yards of rich illusion
a satin stockpile, the bottom

drawer filling with baby clothes.
One's own needlework, restless

fingers failing to be still at the borders
of embroidery, ruffled doilies, pillow tops,

dishcloths, the needlework, counted cross-
stitch off too many inches, every edge

uneven, the perpetual dissection of seams.
It's nearly morning. The bride-to-be

lingers, patient, as a spider dangles
in rafters, cattycorner to a hope

chest disfigured by whittled initials
carved. Her monogram, not another

article, needful of mending
with the knot in the throat

and nape of the neck, finally
a flawless execution.

Teisha Dawn Twomey

For my Father on his Birthday

You don't recall the pony, just the clown
with one leg and how all your friends screamed
when his mask came off. It was only Grandpa

under there making balloon animals
and blowing a kazoo. Grandma baked a cake
with Evel Kneivel on it, but you couldn't bear

the way your mother sliced into a legend.
You refused to eat his star spangled helmet,
couldn't stomach biting the heads off

the animal crackers she offered you.
You had named them: Mountain Gorilla,
Rhino, and Camel. The other kids tore into

them and you trembled as appendages
were fractured by teeth. You escaped inside,
cut the strings off your balloons, bounced them

around, watched as they recoiled until bursting
against the plastered ceiling. Then you cried.
You still hate when people give you presents

then want to watch as you open them.
So you open mine slowly, peel each patch
of tape off the way one pulls a scab,

savoring every moment. I never speak
up, hold my tongue, bite down
on it, whatever's required.

Hometown Decay

Those boys press two fingers against
their overbites, whistle, stray dog's bay.

A skinny puppy eats from my compost,
then trails its hind end across the yard

as I pull up a row of pearly white onions,
tugging them out. They'll make me cry later.

I'm just another local girl in cut offs, bent over,
a garden bed daydreaming: Greg's fuzzy dice

swung from his rearview mirror in synch
with his moans. My face was in a lap,

forehead clinking against the flask,
growing warm between thighs. The hula girl

on Josh's dashboard undulated in time
to his own pale hips rising and falling.

After, he'd huddled close to my breast
like a heavy-eyed newborn. It's a small town.

There's nothing else to do. It's this or a trip
to the meth labs just up the road. Far enough

away so we can't hear every explosion.
We polish the silver, set the table just so,

use only the best china, put cloth napkins
on every lap, then every head goes down

in prayer. Still, the sirens go off, men stand
on porches with their guns unlocked.

Women and children take cover. The boy
whose stick shift is stuck, tips his beer

ninety degrees, emptying the never-ending
road-soda. He wants to see the whole world

overturned the way he is most familiar with it.
The girls too, flipped on their backs in the bed

of his pickup. That puppy's mouth was pasty,
swarmed pale by so many milky worms

latching on. Perfect rows of silent teeth, sunk
deep. I run my tongue over gums, check for rot

in a town full of molars, wedged too far
back to bother reaching for them now.

Casanova's Breakfast

In the North End, you pay dock prices.
You tap the open oysters, check

if they're at their best. They must
respond emphatically, feel heavy,

full in your hand. When you shuck
them, you take care not to spill

the juices, wriggling sharp blade
past hinges, severing, swallowing

raw, four-dozen bivalves, wholly
with their colorless blood. Tiny

three-chambered hearts pumping.
You detach belly from basin.

When it's her turn, you show her
how to put the wide end to mouth,

tip it upward, call her a natural
as she brims with pride, snapping

her head back, brand new
at compliantly unbolting.

Each mouthful slips down effortlessly.
A cluster of oysters is called a *bed*

you whisper. Sometimes there is no way
to know which one envelops

a grain of sand beneath their flesh.
They're faceless, have no lips

to forewarn him, he's on the verge
of destroying something rare.

Teisha Dawn Twomey

Birds

It's abnormal, he said, *to pair*.
Still, I prayed to come back

as a Herring Gull, to know
the transmigration of a Blue Jay.

He crooned shrewd songs, strange lines
of reasoning against queries of eternity:

Few animals would be monogamous
if consciousness survived death. Even fish

refuse to imagine being out of water.
I hear a Northern Shrike's call, the trill

and whistle it makes before skewering prey
on a scrub-bush thorn. This pretty stabbing

will stop me in my tracks, from asking
if it's really over. If it is, I will see it

in your eyes, the way they seem
to dilate, just before you screw me.

Leech at the Base of a Beech Tree

It was not always this way. Scavenging for dead
bullheads a fisher may have left behind, feeding
off sickened bullfrogs dying on the banks.
We had colonies that washed along these shores,
currents carried us along, or else we curled up
like pill bugs, rolled down the hill to hunt

in the leaf litter. We held out, waited
for something worthy to drink from the stream,
for the warm folds we found behind velvet ears
of lambs, young deer, all with blood sweet
like maraschino cherries. Now during dry seasons
we burrow, living off memories of nourishment.

When we scavenge, the most we hope for
is a muddy puddle, to find a tadpole or salamander
in some vernal pool of muck, to suck their cool blood.
But today, writhing at the base of this beech tree,
I can hear the five new wrens hatching
and begin to salivate at the prospect of the sibling

rivalry birds are famous for. I can almost picture
the weakest one pushed over the edge, its pink,
hollow-boned body hitting the forest floor, still balmy
from the warmth of its brethren. How I would find
a crevice between its wing and body, warm
underside to fasten myself at its thickest vein,

all three hundred and sixty of my teeth sunk deep
and scissoring. I might feel the hatchling's heart skip
a beat, seize as the blood is re-routed, begins to flow
backwards, so drunk on plasma and hemoglobin,
I'd swell like a thumb hit with a hammer, turn purple
as a grape ready to burst. I'd sap every last drop

out of the wren, while it was fresh. Only then,
when I detached, curling into my most protective position,
you might see the deep emerald eggs I am carrying
at my belly, the ones you hadn't noticed before,
but perhaps you might understand now, as I retreat
carefully back underground, much gentler.

Birthmarks

Babies can be born with pink patches
at the napes of their necks, called stork bites.
If one appears on the eyelids or forehead

it's fondly called an angel's kiss. There are birthmarks
of all varieties; reddish-blue blemishes fading away
by a child's twelfth birthday. Others ranging in shades

from tan to black; the common mole, or port wine stain
that'll remain all life-long, the spidery web-like bloom
of blood. Some splotches could be mistaken for

well-placed bruises by a school-nurse inspecting
a pair of siblings for lice. The big sister blames her
own botched brow on an heavenly angel's kiss

while her brother accuses an incompetent stork
for his clumsy delivery. Every morning he tugs
on the same grubby shirt, the turtleneck unrolled

up to his ears. This put those screeners at ease.
No need to lose sleep, as far as they can see —
some birthmarks come and go, as they please.

Cheerios

In the morning, we had Cheerios.
I marveled at the full bowl, unfamiliar

spoons and whole grains, too stunned
to notice either nut or honey. Just each tiny loop

a bewildered vowel, burbling: Oh*? Oh? Oh?*
How many times have I been here? Astonished

by how much the heart is like a swinging door
closed then suddenly open again, barefoot

at a table, not my table, speechless.
I had hoped the Cheerios might have more to say,

not the chattiest of cereals. No *snap, crackle*
or *pop*. But then—how appropriate they are

those little Oh's. Each one—
floating like a mind blown away.

Pool Shark

When the game gets too close,
I call the shots out loud.

We practice in a local pool hall
where I am allowed free refills

of Shirley Temples and as many quarters
as I can carry to the jukebox. You tell me

I'm *a real good shot*. On weekends
we take on a team of barfly townies

in some pub over the mountain.
They see that pool cue towering over me.

I bat my wide eyes, 'cause you said they
figure *we'll be an easy enough steal*.

Then scratch on the break, miss the first couple
high balls. I warm up the way you taught me.

Soon we bring it home, banking shots
off the sides, behind our backs. I like to

watch the dropped jaws fall as I tighten up
on the angles, begin sinking one shot

after another. When I demand they pay up
fair and square, my palm looks tiny

under all those greasy bills. You lean back
grinning beneath your handlebar mustache

say, *Girl, you done good.* I want to know
if winning will always be so easy, aiming

with one eye closed, the other focused
on a ball, some shot I was born to sink.

Hannah's Ambry
Addressed by Peninnah

Remember the flurry of starlings
rising above the barn? Silly, you
thought they were a bad omen, a flock

of dark divinations beating drab wings
against the dawn. You were so jarred

by their joyless vigor that you
took cover and have been holed up
in the pantry for several hours.

My dear, you're fond of this
space and the sensible shelving

you can provide for, having a knack
for precision. Your interests
include alphabetizing tin cans

and memorizing expiration dates. Darling,
here nothing goes bad. You promised

homemade preserves last year.
Do you recall this as you're hunched
over and under a shelf of blank labels,

the spools of checked ribbon uncoiled?
Ahead is your stockpile of jelly jars.

Proof you'd had intentions,
still thought you could create
something worthy of being dressed up.

You admitted once you'd liked
the idea of conquering something

wild and snarled. You began harvesting
your first bush, so greenhorn
to reaping, and gleaned the branches

with the softest bare hands those hedges
had ever seen. Its thorns pierced your flesh,

and your palms bled, inciting your fear
of miracles and that Christ was still
deep inside you like this thing

that burned forever but was never
consumed. You waited for that bush

to burst into flames, for the angel
of Yahweh to appear and demand
the removal of your sandals

because, Sugar, you are in the land
of milk and honey. Now, you sit there

barefoot and infertile, gorging yourself
on condensed milk and sweet pickles,
polishing off full mason jars

of candied yams. Sweetheart, you eat
an entire loaf of unleavened bread.

The only host present tonight is the one
you consume wholly, no longer fearful
of sacrifice nor the certainty

that something divine is about to
spring up in your world.

Staring at the Sun

Root yourself in heavy mulch,
sow all ten of your toes

into a shallow trench
and stake yourself upright.

But you will never be
like the sunflower,

its ornate, top-heavy bloom-
face ogling the East at sunrise,

its spiraling gaze as gaudy
and brazen as a chandelier.

They're not that Unusual

Meanwhile, mutant daisies grow
seventy miles from Fukeshima,

Japan where a tsunami caused
a nuclear meltdown. Or so I read

that day I had the nightmare
for the first time. The one

where I'm stringing garlands out of flowers
together as fast as I can, for my daughter

with two heads and only one body.
Before I can ever finish the second chain,

the first strand is torn in two, my child
on the right reaches for her sister's crown

again and again, a siren blares, my girls
cry out and have me wishing that I have

more than two arms, just in time
for all my dreams to come true.

It all happens seventy miles from Fukeshima,
Japan, or so I read or heard somewhere

about the two-headed daisies or daughter
or was it just a single girl, only one stem

to the flowers I continue to string
individually in my nightmares.

Anthem for a Mouse

Springs coming loose, great hammers falling,
the shatter of bones as soft bodies give way.

He was only crawling inside to get warm.
He only needed some bedding, perhaps a crumb

or two, but that bar caught his tiny foot so tight
the flesh was wrenched from the bone and
he had no choice but to tow that gory plank

'round, beneath the rocking chair, listening
to more wires snapping closed, the shifting

of dishes, the nibbling. Last week he startled
the man from his sleep, but that wasn't how
he'd met his maker, nor the quick splintering

of spine or neck, a swift and lucky way to die.
No, he dragged himself room to room, bleeding

-out, just like the animal he was. They threw
his velvety-hide out the nearest window.
Tomorrow won't be any different but pray

it is when the light flips on, scurry
from countertop into breadbox.

Playground

Red Rover, Red Rover,
call me over, hand to wrist.

You clothes lined my throat.
I watched your chubby knees
pumping forward, glad kid

on a swing, under-dogging,
trying to punt my sky, capture

the flag, my knobby knuckles
white, still as mice skulls, trapped
above my head, hollowed me

out, holed up in my skin, hid
then poked fun of my plea,

Olli, olli, oxen free!
My mothballed mouth
silently ajar – a sand box,

a body – the can full of rocks
you tipped without being caught.

Red Rose Tea Figurines

When I pack up the shadow
box, displace each figurine

from snug cubby, I contemplate
how much tea two can share

in seven years. About that time
I reach the glass elephant —

its upturned trunk, a betrayal.
I think it best, all the hammers

belong to you. Something breaks
the surface here. The woman beneath

my bones, with no need for porcelain.
I felt her growing teeth in there.

With no whimper

my arms were swept to the side,
unbent from shrouding

the embarrassed contraction
of my chest, willing body

always securing what it needed
and you, never asking permission

to go on. I lingered upright, lips slack,
easing into fleshy ridges, rich, ruddy

swells, an untidy smile, spread out
as a chain of garish trails got uprooted.

Bloom after bloom of proof, belly
to thigh, a thread of sodden hues

pulled up like sharp purple onions.
You opened the window after, swore

we'd worn out the very air inside.
I could feel myself unwind

in the darkness, the untangled
anticipation of fingers and toes.

My body had ceased wincing,
hands gave up flapping that night,

two sunfish given a good hook through
the gills, the tug that set me still

as a toad in the sun. Once you caught
a moth in with us, green as jade.

It chose to fix its crooked antenna,
intently to the west, settled on that

faulty horizon. Why? Oh, God why?
Who knows why? One gets so bound

in one direction, continues collapsing
with each breath as calm as a millpond.

The First Time was a Math Major

She'd have hives in the morning. Allergic
to wool, which did not matter now, pressed up

against him, the Christmas sweater he'd brought back
from break. She was bare-chested, pretending to know

what he meant by binomial coefficients but it was okay
to smile, nod at the logic. He'd waited long enough

so she let him divide her legs, equation solved.
The problem was resolved over a chair

like an inverted v – between x and y. Equivalent Notations —
she was sideways losing it, knowledgeable she'd been less than

and not greater than serving this simple function.
What power she'd been raised to moaning, *I am so bad*

at math, one hand raised straining *call on me*
call on me. I think I finally have the answer.

In That Hour

I visited my mother as she slept, where the living
might hear us. There, I cradled her, crooning strange,

feral lullabies shared only between dreams
and dropped burial cloths, sung by the feathered

ones who have at last taken to the sky. I watched
over her with new eyes, with the gravity

old-wisdom carries. She felt warmth then, waking
to some far-off melody, a déjà vu, a faint light.

it came off. When I looked in the mirror, all I could see was the shine
had left my skin; my shadow was large on the wall. One morning

I woke too late, used up all the hot water. The ceilings cracked the first time
I called you an asshole, your impersonation of me batting my eyes, the gesture

of an empty vessel. I had a dream that night that I hanged myself
in the kitchen. I was a glass sun catcher in the window. You were watching

me spin, the rays pouring through me. The warmth of August drew near.
We spent the afternoon in our backyard. You held a tin can full of sand

and ash. I tore grass from the yard in great handfuls. I once tried
to sculpt a bust of my favorite artist and the head collapsed into itself.

I saw you then, head in hands, and me smoothing coil
after coil, building you a crown too heavy for your neck.

How to Treat Pretty Things

Our first apartment was located behind a glass shop, appropriate in hindsight.
You were still blowing hot air into me then and holding me up to the light.

Truck smelling like a salt marsh, back from Plum Island, your first gift to me
was a shell. I pressed it to my ear, heard the million waves, saw

our children with tawny wet locks, freckled and coddled, cocooned
by monogrammed beach towels. You spoke my middle name softly, *Dawn*

when you learned it was something that either cracks or breaks on the horizon.
I began to tell stories from childhood, leading you up and down the family

staircases, so you could see each awkward school picture, the chronicled
collections of descending smiles. When you proposed I didn't know

which hand to put forward, so I thrust them both out, hoping you might.
It was April and I was your fool. You pulled my leg so hard,

Ode to the Caesarean

Sometimes my mother tells me I'm getting too old to burrow into her
like this, but mostly she lets me imagine I'm still hidden,

seamlessly bound to her. When she told me about being cut
from hip to hip, I pictured the magic trick where the magician

severs his lovely assistant in half. I wanted to apologize.
Instead, I refused my cousin's hand-me down bikini

in solidarity. My mother and I wear identical black one-pieces
to the beach. When she undresses, I do not get caught peeping

at the ribbon of rosy scar tissue. At night I see her
kneading it with her palm, her slippery fingers covered

in Lubriderm as they work counter-clockwise.
I wonder if it would ache if I disappeared.

Wanderlust

I want to believe in truck stop diners,
blueberry pancakes, vacation villages

on the way to Never-ever-again Land.
By morning, I'd think any place

could be home. I continue to carry
old key chains with me.

They fail to unlock any doors
but open as many cold-ones

as I need. So I call my older brother.
He is always on vacation and I ruin

his good time. He has predictable advice
on the other line: I should really take

care. Tonight I'm smashed-mouthed
and stormy. Sometimes I'm like that

grand illusion destroyed. I want that
tonight. To be unlike me, soft-spoken

and sweet. A child un-
willing to take off

her boots, backpack off,
laces laced too tight.

After being told to keep an eye on his sister

he was curious about how deep
the deep-end was, if she would float

or tread water. She just looked up
at him, chubby fists still clutching the dandelions

she'd plucked poolside, wide eyes fluttering
as if trying to blink Morse code. He rolled her

past the six-foot mark, watched her sink
to the bottom, some lucky penny.

She did not scream then as she does now
when he lowers her into a warm bath,

feels the wetness come, rise past her
now-thick hips, the woman-curves.

Teisha Dawn Twomey

Origami Towels

In Quepos, even before
the early morning

sing-song trill:
rise and shine

buoyed me beyond
my flooding dream

where our bungalow
filled little by little,

seawater rising to thigh,
chest, head, sunk out

with the undertow. I was
sharply shuddered ashore.

Awoke, feet between
two strange birds, twin

terrycloth towels,
the sweet maids wrung

to remind us of swans.
Gliding the crisp linen,

exquisite origami, all
those mute throats.

The Tyrant

You woke too early: Listened to the birds, called back to them.
Easter morning your grandson is beating his fists against the table,

sweaty little tyrant. I've propped his rotund body on one knee,
so he can see you press your grizzled mustache against an eggshell

to teach him, as you taught me, how to blow the innards out
of the ones we want to keep. You used to frighten me;

you enjoyed puzzles, could read maps and a compass.
I never knew which way was East.

You woke too early: Listened to the birds, called back to them.

You'd tried to teach me once: *Old Sam Peabody, Peabody, Peabody,*
who cooks for you? Who cooks for you all? Nonsense, I'd whispered,

copycatting how my mother pitched her hip when I'd heard her call
you Fascist. You were highbrowed, enveloped by thick publications,

always scribbling illegible things, requiring cigarette breaks
and bold coffee. Nana swept ash from the floors just yesterday.

You woke too early: Listened to the birds, called back to them.

And we re-papered the country-chicken wallpaper she'd fallen in
love with thirty years ago, kneeling side-by-side, tearing the roosters

as you chanted in the baby's ear: *Old Sam Peabody,*
Peabody, Peabody, who cooks for you? Who cooks for you all?

Such a carefully gauged whisper, *gentle now* — you crooned,
as if he were a thing you'd wanted to keep.

Hot Potato

I shudder when I call you my darling,
my ruined one. The thing I stopped

completely, easier than cigarettes,
simpler than shoplifting. Gave you up

faster than I could scratch tickets,
the sound of penny scraping the center

of a cartoon shamrock. See? You were
more like me than I'll ever know.

Afterwards, I dropped in on an old friend.
She and I squinted westward, tilting heads

at her life as the twins, redheaded
boys, tottered over a manicured yard.

Their hammed fists shoved a bright ball
forward back and forth, a hot potato

passed over the perfect blades of grass.
One shrieked. The child split my ears.

No, not you, hushed, silent as a squib.
I used to be fearful of growing a fuse

inside, of your curling limbs sprouting
barbs. I never won, my lovely, not a thing

shaking away the fragile jaw, padded
chin, the soft angles left still inside me.

You were my only miracle. Your limp lungs
still as dandelions pulled up from the lawn.

Ninety-Eight Percent
of the Universe is Invisible

Often, we've failed to pay attention
to the inevitable. Now you want to

tell your mother what she has missed.
Begin by staring at the sun. Ask her

if she knows what's really happened.
Millions of stars died for us to be born,

billions of years ago every atom was forged
of this shatter. Inquire whether she's perceived

her own annual turnover of bones. *What we are*
is walking galaxies of fossil stardust. Tell her

of the many skins we've shed along the way
an allegory — *the many children toddling buckets*

towards sandcastles at the seashore. Generations
will continue tunneling their moats deeper

trying to keep out the nightmares, building
barricades, as if the Big Bang's not manifesting

all around us. You cannot protect anything
from this collapse. Instead, fold up her chair,

your beach-blankets at sunset. On the way
back to the car, hold her hand firmly.

Pat her eyes dry. Suspend her disbelief
for a moment, in the comfort of this

each of us is always
on our way back home.

Mixing Business with Pleasure

He speaks of policy, conspicuous
logistics, narrows pale, calculating
eyes she wants to make widen

across the desk. She slouches low,
uncrosses ankles, showing him
that stark sliver of her

which doesn't care about decorum
or propriety. There is not a door
to his office. *If there was,*

he says, *it would be closed now.*
If there was, she still doesn't know
which side of it she'd be on.

On Shame

Crouching on either side of the stone fence,
hours spent buttressing this border, arms full
of limestone and granite. Our backs strained,

necks craned at our divided image, a mirrored
illusion of regret, having been the ones building
this monstrosity all along. Howling in seclusion,

you vowed years ago, *we're all alone.* Now
if I'd believed you, we both would have been,
we could have bayed at the same lone moon

for having forsaken us and awakened
clinging to shame, our hair tangled
in burrs, both missing the untidy morning

glories creeping up and over this division.
There is forgiveness in fervent pursuit of light.
What is natural, clambers to scale the wall.

You seek comfort downhill, flank yourself
between dim walls like clockwork, stacking
cold meat and cheese, making a couple brown bags

out of habit. Open your windows to the un-tillable
tiger lilies, bleeding hearts, forget-me-nots, marigolds
returning perennially, annually, keeping promises.

By mourning, their buds unguarded themselves.
There is absolution all around you. Season after season
behold the blooms appearing, unabashed at being visible.

For my Niece Lauren at Two Weeks Old

Although you are very small, I want you to know:
the bay is a large body of water, your parents

are the coastline. They surround you. Remember
this later, if your own shores seem thin, if ever

you feel stranded. When you are older, I hope
you'll visit the sea often, a good reminder.

Your father and I were both born on Cape Cod.
His eyes, the color of its coastal waters. Notice:

this cape shields the state of Massachusetts
from major storms. The bay is a place

where gifts roll up at your feet. You could
collect them, conch shells especially.

Press them to your ear and you'll hear the waves
deep inside. This too will serve as a reminder

of how strong you are. A bay may be called a gulf,
a cove, a sound. The sound of waves were heard

the moment you were born. I promise
I heard them, saw you curling shoreward.

Don't say you will call tomorrow

to chat about what it is like outside,
the color of the sky, the grey markings

on some kestrel's wing you saw soaring
through the clear blue. I don't want to talk

about the albino animal exhibit you saw
yesterday at a museum. If you must talk

about the weather, let's discuss the habits
of cyclones, those monsters of the ocean

rise to destroy the canopy, carelessly
ripping the deepest roots from the ground.

Those windy brutes do all that work,
only to toss everything aside. Explain

this. If you are going to talk about birds,
let's examine their hunting patterns,

how some appear to hover midair
before plunging steeply downward

and impaling their prey. Articulate
this: The Peregrine Falcon strikes

with all four toes extended and skewers
its victim. You can see the backfire, the spray

of blood, the cloud of feathers when it strikes.
It's like a piñata bursting. If you listen carefully

you can hear the feebler fowl's hollow bones
shattering on impact. Who wouldn't appreciate that?

You celebrate the resourcefulness of the raptor,
how it examines each move, evaluates energy

costs, meticulously weighs risks: action against
inaction, advantages vs. disadvantages, grows wary

of loss. I know both of us can relate.
If I must hear one more thing

about the taxidermy squirrel, then speak
of deficiency; the shortcomings and flaws

that lead to its certified demise. Let's discuss
the intrinsic sightlessness of said defect:

how this one, albinism and color blindness,
are more common in males than females.

Do you think it's a coincidence?
Uniqueness has a heavy price.

Learn to weigh that cost like an accipiter;
what you see as beauty, only makes one

a target for slaughter, decimation. It's a relief
to sidestep idle chit-chat in lieu of metaphors.

The small talk you think keeps you safe,
reminds me only of our nature. Don't play

dumb. It's just like your towheaded squirrel,
poorly camouflaged and giving up it's neck.

What about our defenses, the jaws and claws
we've been hiding for too long? A pleasant face

masks them well, but why bother when bare
bones are the only ones worth mulling over?

That's all that's left between you and me now.
Let's pick at those. The truth is we're born

knowing Cruelty. We imprint onto it —
like a second mother. Let's discuss her.

Contraction

There is a cabinet with no bones,
a tiny dog shrinks at his bowl.

It is bare. If you become small,
you get less of everything.

The cupboard holds onto a wall,
the wall holds down the floor.

The floor has a hole in it.
A trap fills with a cave in

of muscle and bone. The dog kneads,
pawing the hollow drum,

beats, the dog, getting less.
The world's full of this

sound, the humming contraction,
a song of rats throbbing

behind walls, tiny hearts
holding tight to bare cupboards.

Dimples, Take a Bow
for Marilyn

I was nine years old, making nappy rabbits happy.
Never a Shirley Temple, *standin' up there*

*on some stag*e — more culture than age. I knew
what his teacher learned 'im, my mother
with her sexy shoulder, *rollin' loose on a ball joint.*

Copycat his careless words, the new students. A mechanic
with a Mississippi drawl; *nothin' like her city shimmy.*

He mows our lawn *an' crab apple trees give way
for somethin' else* — has got to give. *Don't say nothin'
to no one*, about the weekends, holidays, the momentum

of him *pushin' your bike, 'til you better pedal, better pedal
faster, up and o'er yonder mountain*, making

those nappy rabbits happy. Never a Shirley Temple.
I've practiced the courtesy of curtsy, *but y'are what y'are,
another rollin' shoulder, an apple not rollin' far* enough.

Lead a horse to water — *that tall drink of water.*
I swear, she always drinks. She will always drink.

Moment Before, Moment After
for the hibakusha *

The ten thousand suns scattered
her universe, four goldfish bellied-up

towards the light, then glimmered
into dust. She stood in a shallow tide

plucking lily-white skeletons —
keyhole sand dollars from the shore.

She'd halved them, unfettered from each
five tiny doves of peace hidden inside.

A red-crowned crane sat on her nest
of two broken yolks. Krishna turned

his back, his blue-lotus skin passing
them by, as the sound of flutes faded

the reversed silhouettes stained the walls.
His ocean of mercy scattered in a whirlpool

of thirst. Her fingertips caught first, molten
flesh trailing light gray down her wrists

before both elbows ignited. The finale
of the fallen curtain preluded, just

three colors: red, black, brown — was all
this child saw, as her little brother tore

ahead in the dark, his delicate ankles
tugged past her outstretched arms.

Can you hear the bells the children ring?
Bowing, deeply in her direction, they wince

at the sky, considering all the shadows
refusing to be washed away.

* In Japan, *hibakusha* literally translates to "bomb-affected people." Following the
atomic explosions at Hiroshima and Nagasaki in 1945, the Japanese began to use this
word to describe the victims who witnessed and survived the horror of these attacks.

Counting on the Cure-All

Put a raw steak on it or try a cure all — soak a cotton ball
in apple cider vinegar, dab the latest swelling circumference.

Rub black pepper or honey, massage vigorously, whatever
old wives tale you can believe. Manage to maintain something,

a false configuration — control bloom and wane of habitual bruises,
the patterns with their familiar vicinity and rate of recurrence.

The shadow of the paddled boar bristle brush, mark of brass buckle
four fingers, thick thumb, spread wide-open hand, measure the height

and width, an outline eight by four inches, about right for the average
man's hand. Pretty much all this child needs to know about a grown man

is his fist's presumed speed — 20 to 30 mph. It takes eleven pounds
per square inch to choke an adult, for a child, even less — two fingers

of whisky, two thumbs above the brother's voice box. Encode
the gathered data, find logic in the face of horror, count down

the protracted seconds, shades the sibling's face turns, an array
of colors — a contusion turning red to mauve. Count on Monday

coming and count on playing cool at school. Count on the brother
popping his collar up — count on the sister keeping her mouth shut.

He's been blue thirty seconds, she won't count him out cold.
Count on some cure all, black pepper or honey, last two fingers

of whiskey, bottle neck massage, thumbs working, counter
clockwise, put a steak on it, move contusions backwards

in time. He will wake, count on it, count on a cure-all, and manage to
maintain some false configuration. Count on Monday coming.

A Triptych of Unhinging Certainties

"Be empty of worrying. Think of who created thought!
Why do you stay in prison, when the door is so wide open?"
— Rumi

Part I

Bird's knees appear to bend backward.
You're actually seeing long ankles

off the ground, roughly positioned
where one expects our own joints

to fold. Fallibility is everywhere.
Intelligence is a relative thing.

You don't need to be that smart
or strong. You don't have to be fast.

Just be smarter, or stronger, or faster
than your competition. What is *happy*?

Make an educated guess. Fashion a weapon
from rock and wood, control fire, conform.

Use complex language.
Who asked the first question?

Part II

The first time I asked a question
in a poem, I realized you were there

listening. Also, these words weren't mine.
Am I still trying to respond to the original

inquiry? I assume it sounded like a cry
for milk — communicated basic need.

We can unearth new fossils everyday.
I derive all else from experience.

If you can't rid yourself of the fossils in your closet,
you might as well teach those bones to dance.

Part III

Pick one, an emotion. Fact is, with animals, fear
is the easiest to determine. How can you really tell

whether rabbit or rat is happy? It's much easier to test alarm.
A resonating tone warns an animal it's to receive a shock.

The amygdalae — those two little lumps of grey
matter (one in each hemisphere of the brain) respond.

We're not privy to everything we've "seen."
This secret knowledge has us flinching at the unexpected.

With little to go on, we bend everything backwards, twisting
truth on its head. What's beneath these lines?

A hollow bell, which won't stop ringing for anything.
It communicates basic need — sounds like a cry for milk.

Saving Face

When you have dried toothpaste on your chin,
I don't tell you anymore. I let you go

to the office with bran between your teeth,
toast crumbs on the crotch of your khakis.

Sometimes I reach for you, as if by impulse,
then pretend to be shielding my own face

from the sun. You're not any better.
On our anniversary, you don't tell me

I've tucked my skirt into my nylons.
I have lipstick on my teeth. On my shoe,

I trail along toilet paper on the way back
from the bathroom. We've grown tired

of looking after the smaller things:
eyelashes, which have fallen

on one other's cheeks. We don't giggle
out of embarrassment for each other

anymore. I wish I could let you know
your reading glasses are still on your head,

Silly. You run around the house
flipping couch cushions and cursing

at our dog for being under your feet
all the time. I whisper the old Seeing Eye

game we used to play, *Darling,*
you're getting cold, no colder,

even colder. You are frozen, goddamn it!
Why don't you just look in the mirror?

After a Quote by Viktor Frankl *

I've been fitting back together for years,
your premeditations too muddled for me
to consume myself with a single match,

the simple purpose. I liked watching it
burn, the flame licking your fingertips,
daring them to continue pressing together,

stubborn head bowing low as you refused
breath, the brushfire you began on the horizon
in dry fields smoldered bare-bone by daybreak.

How could I forgive myself for not resisting
such fiery willpower, stopping the consummation,
the valley erupting, every brook left gasping?

Smoke billowed 'til morning, proof you'd been
here, like muddy boot prints I'd known you
to leave behind, brandishing the floors, any place

your hat hung awhile. You unwrapped a parcel
of magnesium, showed me how to hold that
little blond stone, catch a spark in fine tinder,

coerce the shyest core of heat from dry husk
and twigs. I still allow myself this solo pleasure,
remembering your pockets full of coal,

glazed in gasoline, striking that last match forward,
unshaken as a moth, gracefully beating its wings
black against the glow, suddenly reborn.

* *"What is to give light must endure burning."* ~Victor Frankl

Natural History

I know the false description of evolution:
the slow march of amoeba to man,

a sequence of progressing complexity.
Natural history is a pageant of disarticulation

punctuated by mass extinction. The universe's tendency
is towards collapse. In any case, grasp a fossil, a shadow

of its past, take the nautilus, a chambered cephalopod.
We hold up the shell and try to show its growth

is relative to the moral development of man.
Our work is small. We'll see what we want to see.

Forge a fortress out of a bombed out refuge
I don't know any other way but this —

After all, there's still art on the walls.

A female Redback

Spider looms her tough untidy web,
another male offers up his abdomen,

somersaulting towards her mouthparts
in exchange for a moment or two close

to her. This vulnerable posture only elicits
a predatory response. The smaller he is,

the more forceful he'll be cannibalized.
This first and last instinctual barter

beneficial to the species mutually.
He doesn't consider the pros and cons.

He's driven towards her snare, the dance
in his loins, a never-ending Congo

of brothers to come after and before,
lined up at her door. She tidies her untidy

trap, never waits long. Same old song
on the radio. A young woman practices

tying slipknots behind her double-bolted
door. The female Redback Spider has it

pretty good. Not just a girl in this country
town, has powerful limbs, a set of fangs,

no step-daddy too young for the mother
but not the daughter. The female bares

a bright blaze on its abdomen.
It warns: don't draw too close.

You're sure to lose a hand.
That's just how it is, plain as day,

seems fair and square. Her venom
could kill a full-grown man.

Acknowledgments

Special thanks to the editors of the following publications in which these poems, some of which have been revised, first appeared:

Fried Chicken and Coffee: "Coming Home," "Memory of a Pool Shark," "Lamentation of the Mouse," "Wanderlust," "A female Redback"

Ibbetson Street Press: "How to Treat Pretty Things," "Hannah's Ambry," "Saving Face," "Moment Before, Moment After," Counting on the Cure-All," "They're not that Unusual," "Natural History"

The Common Ground Review: "Ninety-Eight Percent of the Universe is Invisible," "The Tyrant," "Self-Portrait at Age Seventy-Nine"

The Main Street Rag: "For My Father on his Birthday"

Sante Fe Literary Review: "For my Niece Lauren at Two Weeks Old"

Contemporary American Voices: "Contraction"

New Graffiti: "Hometown Decay"

Poetica: "Leech at the Base of a Beech Tree"

Much gratitude to the guidance of the many wonderful teachers and mentors I've had along the way, including Ruth Post, Thomas Laier, George Parrino, Marlis Paffenroth, Abbot Cutler, Jeff McRae, David Langston, J.D. Scrimgeour, Teresa Cader, and Bonnie Bishoff. Grateful acknowledgement to Lesley University's MFA program and the talented members of my cohort. Also, I am thankful for the friendships of Tierney Rosenstock, Michael Gromacki, Mary Benson, Shari Caplan, Robert Krantz, Erica Sheline, and my little editor, Lily Mumford. I would also like to extend my heartfelt appreciation to Timothy Gager, Stephanie Blackman, Rusty Barnes, Lawrence Kessenich, Steve Glines, January Gill O'Neil, Meg Tuite, James R. Whitley, Doug Holder, Lo Gallucio, Harris Gardner, Rene Schwiesow, David Miller, Chad Parenteau, Blaine Hebel, Tony Toledo, Christopher Reilley, Robin Stratton, Gloria Mindock, Sudasi J. Clement, Donald Vincent, Clay Ventre, M.P. Carver, and Enzo Silon Surin. Thank you to my family, especially the love and support of my father, my mother and Dan, my grandparents, my big brother Connan, as well as Terrin, Lauren, and Dawn Twomey.

About the Author

TEISHA DAWN TWOMEY received her MFA in Poetry at Lesley University. She is the poetry editor for Wilderness House Literary Review. Her fiction, nonfiction, and poetry have appeared in numerous print, as well as online, poetry publications. She lives in Boston, M.A.

www.ingramcontent.com/pod-product-compliance
Lightning Source LLC
Chambersburg PA
CBHW032059040426

42449CB00007B/1147